Holt Literature & Language Arts
Introductory Course

PROGRESS ASSESSMENT
Holt Handbook
English-Language Conventions
Tests and Answer Key

Chapter Tests for
- **Grammar**
- **Usage**
- **Mechanics**
- **Sentences**

HOLT, RINEHART AND WINSTON
A Harcourt Classroom Education Company

Austin • New York • Orlando • Atlanta • San Francisco • Boston • Dallas • Toronto • London

STAFF CREDITS

EDITORIAL

Manager of Editorial Operations
Bill Wahlgren

Executive Editor
Robert R. Hoyt

Project Editor
Randy Dickson

Writing and Editing
Gail Coupland, Amber M. Rigney, *Associate Editors*

Copyediting
Michael Neibergall, *Copyediting Manager;* Mary Malone, *Copyediting Supervisor;* Joel Bourgeois, Elizabeth Dickson, Emily Force, Julie A. Hill, Julia Thomas Hu, Jennifer Kirkland, Millicent Ondras, Dennis Scharnberg, *Copyeditors*

Project Administration
Marie Price, *Managing Editor;* Lori De La Garza, *Editorial Operations Coordinator;* Heather Cheyne, Mark Holland, Marcus Johnson, Jennifer Renteria, Janet Riley, Kelly Tankersley, *Project Administration;* Ruth Hooker, Joie Pickett, Margaret Sanchez, *Word Processing*

Editorial Permissions
Janet Harrington, *Permissions Editor*

ART, DESIGN AND PHOTO
Graphic Services
Kristen Darby, Manager
Jeff Robinson, *Senior Ancillary Designer*

Image Acquisitions
Joe London, *Director;* Jeannie Taylor, *Photo Research Supervisor;* Tim Taylor, *Photo Research Supervisor;* Rick Benavides, *Photo Researcher;* Cindy Verheyden, *Senior Photo Researcher,* Elaine Tate, *Supervisor*

Cover Design
Curtis Riker, *Director*
Sunday Patterson, *Designer*

PRODUCTION/ MANUFACTURING
Belinda Barbosa Lopez, *Senior Production Coordinator*
Carol Trammel, *Production Supervisor*
Beth Prevelige, *Senior Production Manager*

Copyright © by Holt, Rinehart and Winston

All rights reserved. No part of this publication may be reproduced or transmitted in any form or by any means, electronic or mechanical, including photocopy, recording, or any information storage and retrieval system, without permission in writing from the publisher.

Teachers using HOLT LITERATURE AND LANGUAGE ARTS may photocopy blackline masters in complete pages in sufficient quantities for classroom use only and not for resale.

Printed in the United States of America
ISBN 0-03-066081-5

12345 022 04 03 02 01

Table of Contents

About These Tests iv

Chapter 1 Test: The Sentence 1

Chapter 2 Test: Parts of Speech Overview
Noun, Pronoun, Adjective 3

Chapter 3 Test: Parts of Speech Overview
Verb, Adverb, Preposition, Conjunction, Interjection 5

Chapter 4 Test: The Phrase and the Clause 7

Chapter 5 Test: Complements 9

Chapter 6 Test: Agreement 11

Chapter 7 Test: Using Verbs Correctly 13

Chapter 8 Test: Using Pronouns Correctly 15

Chapter 9 Test: Using Modifiers Correctly 17

Chapter 10 Test: A Glossary of Usage 19

Chapter 11 Test: Capital Letters 21

Chapter 12 Test: Punctuation
End Marks, Commas, Semicolons, Colons 23

Chapter 13 Test: Punctuation
Underlining (Italics), Quotation Marks, Apostrophes,
Hyphens, Parentheses 25

Chapter 14 Test: Spelling 27

Chapter 15 Test: Correcting Common Errors 29

Chapter 16 Test: Writing Effective Sentences 31

Answer Key 35

Answer Sheet, for tests in this booklet 41

Correcting Common Errors Test Answer Sheet,
for tests in Chapter 15 of the *Holt Handbook* 42

FOR THE TEACHER
About These Tests

Tests | This booklet contains chapter tests for the first sixteen chapters of the *Introductory Course Holt Handbook*. Each test, which is presented in the multiple-choice format of a standardized test, gives you a means for assessing your students' grasp of key English language conventions taught in grade six. After you complete instruction on a specific chapter from the *Holt Handbook*, copy a class set of the corresponding chapter test and the appropriate answer sheet contained in this booklet; then, administer the test.

Answer Key | When testing is complete, score each test by using the answer key at the back of this booklet. For all tests, the answer key indicates the correct answers and provides useful references that tie these answers to the relevant *Holt Handbook* instruction. For the grammar, usage, and mechanics tests, the answer key also provides instructional references for all incorrect answer choices. These references will help you pinpoint which skills and concepts students have mastered and which skills and concepts need further attention.

The Sentence: Subject and Predicate, Kinds of Sentences

CHAPTER TEST

DIRECTIONS Read each sentence below. For items 1–6, choose the answer that identifies each underlined word or group of words. For items 7–10, choose the answer that identifies the kind of sentence.

EXAMPLES

1. Will <u>Eli</u> or <u>Al</u> sleep on the top bunk?
   A sentence
   B compound verb
   C compound subject
   D complete predicate

   Answer Ⓐ Ⓑ ⬤ Ⓓ

2. What an interesting person she is!
   A interrogative
   B exclamatory
   C declarative
   D imperative

   Answer Ⓐ ⬤ Ⓒ Ⓓ

---

1. Without any help, my little sister Mary <u>lifted</u> the heavy box.
   A simple subject
   B complete predicate
   C compound subject
   D simple predicate, or verb

2. Every year <u>the Arapaho</u> held a Sun Dance celebration.
   A sentence
   B simple subject
   C complete subject
   D complete predicate

3. <u>At the age of four</u>, the artist Wang Yani <u>exhibited her art</u>.
   A simple predicate, or verb
   B complete predicate
   C sentence
   D complete subject

4. Before breakfast, Grandma <u>writes</u> in her journal and <u>walks</u> a mile.
   A compound verb
   B simple subject
   C complete predicate
   D compound subject

5. After a delay of nearly an hour, the <u>line</u> began to move.
   A simple predicate, or verb
   B complete subject
   C simple subject
   D sentence

GO ON

Chapter Tests

1

for CHAPTER 1 page 2 *continued*   CHAPTER TEST

6. My <u>dog</u> and the neighbor's <u>cat</u> like to play together.
   A complete predicate
   B complete subject
   C compound verb
   D compound subject

7. What an exciting finish that was!
   A exclamatory
   B imperative
   C interrogative
   D declarative

8. The capital of Iceland is Reykjavik.
   A exclamatory
   B declarative
   C imperative
   D interrogative

9. Count to twenty, and open your eyes.
   A imperative
   B interrogative
   C exclamatory
   D declarative

10. Did Isaac Bashevis Singer write the short story "Zlateh the Goat"?
    A exclamatory
    B imperative
    C declarative
    D interrogative

Parts of Speech Overview: Noun, Pronoun, Adjective

for CHAPTER 2 *page 24*

CHAPTER TEST

DIRECTIONS Read each sentence below. Then, choose the answer that identifies each underlined word or group of words.

EXAMPLE

1. We bought stamps at the <u>post office</u>.
   A pronoun
   B proper adjective
   C adjective
   D noun

   Answer Ⓐ Ⓑ Ⓒ ●

---

1. This <u>snake</u> is not poisonous.
   A proper noun
   B pronoun
   C common noun
   D adjective

2. Have <u>you</u> ever tasted Chinese mooncakes?
   A pronoun
   B common noun
   C proper adjective
   D proper noun

3. The <u>eager</u> children lined up at the door.
   A proper adjective
   B adjective
   C proper noun
   D common noun

4. The video game about famous artists is <u>mine</u>.
   A common noun
   B adjective
   C proper noun
   D pronoun

5. Mr. Garza looks <u>tired</u> today.
   A noun
   B pronoun
   C adjective
   D proper adjective

GO ON

Chapter Tests   3

for CHAPTER 2 page 24 continued

CHAPTER TEST

6. One of the best-known Hindu gods is <u>Krishna</u>.
   A   common noun
   B   proper noun
   C   proper adjective
   D   pronoun

7. <u>This</u> is the latest book written by Phyllis Shalant.
   A   proper noun
   B   pronoun
   C   proper adjective
   D   adjective

8. Grandfather taught me a <u>Nigerian</u> folk song.
   A   proper adjective
   B   pronoun
   C   adjective
   D   proper noun

9. Justin brought <u>these</u> snacks to share with the class.
   A   pronoun
   B   common noun
   C   proper noun
   D   demonstrative adjective

10. Did you tell <u>anyone</u> your password?
   A   noun
   B   adjective
   C   pronoun
   D   proper adjective

Parts of Speech Overview: Verb, Adverb, Preposition, Conjunction, Interjection

DIRECTIONS Read each sentence below. Then, choose the answer that identifies each underlined word or group of words.

EXAMPLE

1. Germany, Austria, Italy, <u>and</u> France border Switzerland.
   A conjunction
   B linking verb
   C preposition
   D interjection

   Answer (A) (B) (C) (D)

---

1. Did you look <u>under</u> the bed?
   A adverb
   B conjunction
   C preposition
   D helping verb

2. Rosa <u>usually</u> finishes her homework before supper.
   A transitive verb
   B intransitive verb
   C conjunction
   D adverb

3. Pianist Claude Bolling <u>combines</u> classical and jazz music.
   A action verb
   B linking verb
   C interjection
   D conjunction

4. <u>Wow</u>! This tortilla soup is delicious!
   A adverb
   B interjection
   C conjunction
   D transitive verb

5. <u>Soon</u> the taxi will arrive.
   A interjection
   B linking verb
   C action verb
   D adverb

GO ON

6. You may use my scissors, but please return them.
   A preposition
   B linking verb
   C conjunction
   D adverb

7. The Millersville Puppet Theater will perform tonight in the high school auditorium.
   A prepositional phrase
   B verb phrase
   C interjection
   D conjunction

8. My uncle is the Web-page editor for the National Cartoonists Society.
   A action verb
   B helping verb
   C conjunction
   D linking verb

9. The bumps behind a toad's eyes produce a protective poison.
   A preposition
   B conjunction
   C verb
   D interjection

10. The chess club meets in the cafeteria after school.
    A linking verb
    B helping verb
    C intransitive verb
    D transitive verb

| NAME | CLASS | DATE | SCORE |

for **CHAPTER 4** page 74

CHAPTER TEST

The Phrase and the Clause: Prepositional Phrases, Independent and Subordinate Clauses, Sentence Structure

DIRECTIONS Read each sentence below. For items 1–6, choose the answer that identifies each underlined word or group of words. For items 7–10, choose the answer that identifies the structure of each sentence.

EXAMPLES

1. <u>I will meet you outside</u> when the bell rings.
   A adjective phrase
   B adverb phrase
   C independent clause
   D subordinate clause
   Answer

2. Hoy uses chopsticks when he eats rice.
   A simple
   B compound
   C compound-complex
   D complex
   Answer

1. The classical music <u>on this CD</u> relaxes me.
   A adjective phrase
   B adverb phrase
   C adjective clause
   D adverb clause

2. <u>Without a sound</u>, Lee tiptoed up the stairs.
   A subordinate clause
   B adverb phrase
   C independent clause
   D adjective phrase

3. <u>If we win tonight's game</u>, we will be the district champions!
   A adjective clause
   B adjective phrase
   C adverb phrase
   D adverb clause

4. While Joel was in India, <u>he visited the Taj Mahal</u>.
   A adjective phrase
   B adverb phrase
   C independent clause
   D subordinate clause

GO ON

for **CHAPTER 4** page 74 continued

CHAPTER TEST

5. Did Sharon Creech win a Newbery Medal <u>for her book *Walk Two Moons*</u>?
   A prepositional phrase
   B independent clause
   C adjective clause
   D adverb clause

6. Do you know the name of the artist <u>who painted this series of paintings</u>?
   A prepositional phrase
   B adjective clause
   C independent clause
   D adverb clause

7. Our bird feeder attracts many different birds, but wrens are my favorite.
   A compound
   B simple
   C compound-complex
   D complex

8. Elayne wrote and illustrated a safety manual for baby sitters.
   A compound-complex
   B compound
   C simple
   D complex

9. We painted the wall white, and after it dried, we painted a beautiful rainbow.
   A simple
   B complex
   C compound
   D compound-complex

10. Jodi listened to music on headphones while Marcus finished his homework.
    A simple
    B compound-complex
    C compound
    D complex

for **CHAPTER 5** page 104

CHAPTER TEST

Complements: Direct and Indirect Objects, Subject Complements

DIRECTIONS Read each sentence below. Then, identify each underlined word or group of words according to its use in the sentence.

EXAMPLE

1. The heart pumps <u>blood</u> to all parts of the body.
   A   direct object
   B   indirect object
   C   predicate nominative
   D   predicate adjective

   Answer

1. Coach West gave her <u>players</u> a pep talk at halftime.
   A   direct object
   B   predicate nominative
   C   indirect object
   D   predicate adjective

2. Your forehead feels <u>warm</u>.
   A   predicate nominative
   B   predicate adjective
   C   direct object
   D   indirect object

3. A hexagon is a <u>figure</u> with six sides.
   A   direct object
   B   predicate nominative
   C   indirect object
   D   predicate adjective

4. I need <u>beets</u> and <u>potatoes</u> for this Russian potato salad.
   A   compound predicate adjective
   B   compound indirect object
   C   compound predicate nominative
   D   compound direct object

5. Jerome Tiger became a famous American Indian <u>artist</u>.
   A   predicate nominative
   B   direct object
   C   indirect object
   D   predicate adjective

GO ON

Chapter Tests   9

for **CHAPTER 5** page 104 continued

CHAPTER TEST

6. Do you know the <u>answer</u> to this question?
   A predicate adjective
   B direct object
   C predicate nominative
   D indirect object

7. Miss Jones offered <u>Gary</u> and <u>me</u> some help with our Web-page design.
   A compound indirect object
   B compound direct object
   C compound predicate adjective
   D compound predicate nominative

8. Mai will be the student-council <u>president</u> next year.
   A predicate adjective
   B indirect object
   C direct object
   D predicate nominative

9. Grandma sent us a <u>postcard</u> from New Zealand.
   A indirect object
   B direct object
   C predicate nominative
   D predicate adjective

10. My new dress is <u>fashionable</u> but <u>inexpensive</u>.
    A compound predicate nominative
    B compound direct object
    C compound predicate adjective
    D compound indirect object

Agreement: Subject and Verb, Pronoun and Antecedent

for **CHAPTER 6** *page 122*

CHAPTER TEST

DIRECTIONS Read each set of sentences. Three of the sentences in each set have errors in agreement; one sentence is written correctly. Choose the sentence that is written correctly, with NO ERRORS in agreement.

> **EXAMPLE**
>
> 1. A Where is the snacks?
>   B Several of the travelers lost his luggage.
>   C Someone forgot to close his or her locker.
>   D Bob don't have an e-mail address.
>
> Answer Ⓐ Ⓑ ● Ⓓ

1. A Tony play the cello in the school orchestra.
   B Few of the horses is wearing saddles.
   C My brother or I delivers the morning newspaper.
   D The bride and the groom opened their presents.

2. A Most lizards live in hot, dry regions.
   B Don't she sing Latin music?
   C Here is the costumes for tonight's performance.
   D None of the passengers lost his or her luggage.

3. A Several of the students brings lunches from home.
   B Aunt Sita are preparing a spicy Indian dish called *dal*.
   C Ducks and geese usually flies in V-formation.
   D Elsa or Jill will bring her volleyball to the picnic.

4. A The city council members is voting on housing improvements.
   B All of my sisters sings in the choir.
   C There are over 3,000 islands around Korea's coastline.
   D Neither his ankle nor his knee have healed completely.

5. A Either Carlos or Chen will show us his vacation pictures.
   B The auditorium seat over 500 people.
   C These mats from Madagascar is woven by hand.
   D A pencil and paper is all you need for the test.

GO ON

Chapter Tests

11

6.
A Sorry, Pam, but we wasn't listening when you gave the directions.
B Many of my classmates volunteer within the community.
C Neither of the boys brought their notebook.
D This dress don't fit me anymore.

7.
A One of these skateboards belong to Anna.
B Red eyes, a runny nose, and a headache is all symptoms of allergies.
C Each of the girls braided their own hair.
D Three colorful hand towels hang on the towel rack in the guest bathroom.

8.
A Maria and Joel don't eat sweets.
B Each of my questions were answered.
C The Cossack dancers from Russia is famous for their strong, high kicks.
D That hat and jacket doesn't belong to me.

9.
A Mike and Elvin visited his relatives in Canada.
B Both of the women bought her tickets at the box office.
C Many of our Jewish neighbors celebrates Hanukkah.
D Nobody in our class read his or her essay aloud.

10.
A Mrs. Cly or Miss Hoffman will take their class on a field trip.
B Boxes of donated food arrives daily at the homeless shelter.
C Neither of these stories was written by Lensey Namioka.
D As a snack, raisins or a banana boost my energy.

Using Verbs Correctly: Principal Parts, Regular and Irregular Verbs, Tense

DIRECTIONS Read each set of sentences below. Three of the sentences in each set have errors in verb usage; one sentence is written correctly. Choose the sentence that is written correctly, with NO ERRORS in verb usage.

EXAMPLE

1. A He walked across the room and opens the door.
   B How many times has Alberto Salazar winned the New York Marathon?
   C Dana has broke the school's free-throw shooting record.
   D I laid your notebook beside the phone.

   Answer Ⓐ Ⓑ Ⓒ ●

---

1. A She has gave you good advice.
   B My family has planned a Colorado backpacking trip.
   C I have been setting by the fire.
   D Jumping the fence, the dog hurted its leg.

2. A I am laying the costume on the chair.
   B Have you ever drank carrot juice?
   C On the Internet, Ed finded a helpful online dictionary.
   D Mary has play drums for two years.

3. A Have gas prices raised since last week?
   B I already ask Monica for directions.
   C Carefully set the Chinese vase on this stand.
   D When she helps with the laundry, she sorted the clothes.

4. A While in Guatemala, we seen a rain forest.
   B Mother braids my hair before I went to school.
   C Pedro has went to the library.
   D Will you raise the high jump bar another inch?

5. A We visited Brazil for the annual festival of Carnival.
   B I knowed that Angela Chen was a good pianist.
   C Hurry! The bell has already rang.
   D The conductor is rising her baton.

GO ON

for CHAPTER 7 page 146 continued

CHAPTER TEST

6. A On vacation, they drove along the California coastline.
    B How long has your sweater lain here?
    C The child's balloon bursted.
    D I passed the ball to Devon, but she looks away.

7. A Has Janusz Korczak wrote any books besides *King Matt the First*?
    B I have never set in such a comfortable chair!
    C Grandpa has swam in the Senior Olympics.
    D The members of Congress have risen to greet the President.

8. A Ben has never ate *kimchi*, a spicy, Korean cabbage dish.
    B Please sit the bag of fruit on the table.
    C As the moon rises, we row toward shore.
    D Alice played the guitar, and Flora sings.

9. A The whirling dervishes from Turkey are supposed to dance tonight.
    B Leah has never ran the 100-yard dash.
    C Our cat enjoys laying in the sun.
    D Emma Lazarus writes the poem that was inscribed on the Statue of Liberty.

10. A Mother use to be an electrician.
    B Is the principal setting in the front row?
    C The American Indian dancer has laid her shawl on the ground.
    D As my favorite artist I have chose Diego Rivera.

Using Pronouns Correctly: Subject and Object Forms

for CHAPTER 8 page 176

CHAPTER TEST

DIRECTIONS Read each set of sentences below. Three of the sentences in each set have errors in pronoun usage; one sentence is written correctly. Choose the sentence that is written correctly, with NO ERRORS in pronoun usage.

EXAMPLE

1. A The speakers were Maya Angelou and her.
   B Sara and him grow organic vegetables.
   C Whom did you choose for your partner?
   D I built a dollhouse for Molly and she.

   Answer (A) (B) **(C)** (D)

1. A Us and them filled the bird feeders.
   B Will Grandma take they and we on a helicopter ride?
   C I will ride behind she and you.
   D Ira read us a story by Gary Soto.

2. A Us sixth graders volunteered at the food bank.
   B They are always welcome here.
   C Did you give Shandra or she the envelope?
   D It was her on the telephone.

3. A For whom did you write this note?
   B Miss Okada showed Ann and she some Japanese poetry cards.
   C Aunt Elsa and her joined the Peace Corps.
   D Did you ask Rick and they for directions?

4. A Please help Jim and I with our project.
   B The only French-speaking people at the party were we.
   C Mrs. Smith offered Alex and he a baby-sitting job.
   D Paul is teaching Betty and I a traditional Kiowa dance.

5. A By who was this dress designed?
   B Mr. Lopez plays tennis with Pete and me.
   C Trevor's family and us celebrate the Jewish holiday Yom Kippur.
   D It could have been them in that blue car.

GO ON

Chapter Tests

15

for CHAPTER 8 page 176 continued   CHAPTER TEST

6. **A** Bob sent Mother and I postcards from Switzerland.
   B Us girls listen to Celtic harp music.
   C Do you know whom the composer of the opera *Don Giovanni* was?
   D The crowd welcomed the governor and him.

7. **A** Two famous women inventors are Madame C. J. Walker and she.
   B The coach thanked Pam and she for helping.
   C Hannah sat in the front between Bert and I.
   D Us bus riders will be late today.

8. **A** Aunt Edith invited you and I to tea.
   B The gallery displayed the African sculptures of Gladman Zinyeka and she.
   C Did you tell the nurse or her about your sore throat?
   D My brothers and me take turns cooking dinner.

9. **A** While in the Philippines, we boys learned to play bamboo flutes.
   B The winners of the math contest are us!
   C Our school's Web page was designed by Kris and he.
   D I fixed Laura and they a Costa Rican dish.

10. **A** Who did the teacher help first?
    B My favorite poets are Luis Omar Salinas and him.
    C Does Lian or she know many Chinese words?
    D Mother praised Kim and I for our good manners.

Using Modifiers Correctly: Comparison and Placement

DIRECTIONS Read each set of sentences below. Three of the sentences in each set have errors in modifier usage; one sentence is written correctly. Choose the sentence that is written correctly, with NO ERRORS in modifier usage.

EXAMPLE

1. A My locker is more messier than yours.
   B The highest mountain peak in Mexico is Pico de Orizaba.
   C Please follow my directions careful.
   D Hungry, the fruit salad looked delicious!

   Answer Ⓐ ● Ⓒ Ⓓ

1. A Manuel Lopez plays the guitar well.
   B After midnight she became sleepily.
   C Can't you find no books about Kwanzaa?
   D The last math problem was the most easiest.

2. A I haven't never visited that Web site.
   B This is the most happiest day of my life!
   C Wash good behind your ears.
   D Of all the animals in this wildlife park, this lion makes the most noise.

3. A Apples and cheese taste well together.
   B A girl is knocking on our door in a red cape.
   C The male cardinal is more colorful than the female.
   D Plant the flowers in the most sunniest spot.

4. A Which of the three jokes is funnier?
   B Mrs. Gold doesn't feel well today.
   C The children walked quiet to the assembly.
   D Before Dally's report, I didn't know nothing about the island of Madagascar.

5. A Do you feel nervously about your part in the play?
   B Give the plate of food to Tony that is wrapped in foil.
   C Alaska is the larger state in the United States.
   D Of the two astronauts, Mae C. Jemison is more experienced.

for **CHAPTER 9** page 196 continued

CHAPTER TEST

6. A Lien hasn't never seen the Great Wall of China.
   B The special report about water pollution interested us.
   C Blanca's Cinco de Mayo costume is more fancier than mine.
   D Did you sleep good during the thunderstorm?

7. A Playing this computer game is more harder than just watching television.
   B Couldn't nobody fix the leaky faucet?
   C Lisa pitched good in the first inning.
   D The song that you just heard was written by Tish Hinojosa.

8. A Juan taught us to dance the *merengue*, who was born in the Dominican Republic.
   B Isn't nobody going to the pool today?
   C Marie can easily run a mile in eight minutes.
   D Do you speak Hindi as good as your brother?

9. A Carol plays tennis more skillfully than I.
   B I gave that poster to my best friend on the wall.
   C Which of the two tacos tastes best?
   D Of all these books, I liked Yoshiko Uchida's *Jar of Dreams* better.

10. A Confused, I asked the teacher to explain.
    B Which of the twins has the best grades?
    C We can't hardly taste the cinnamon in these rolls.
    D The skateboard belongs to Kay with the gold wheels.

A Glossary of Usage: Common Usage Problems

DIRECTIONS Read each set of sentences. Three of the sentences in each set have errors in formal, standard usage; one sentence is written correctly. Choose the sentence that is written correctly, with NO ERRORS in formal, standard usage.

EXAMPLE

1. A Take a towel when you go to the pool.
   B Even though I just ate, I feel kind of hungry.
   C Javier is learning us a Mexican song called "La Cucaracha."
   D Who's coat is this?

   Answer

1. A The author Pat Mora ain't from Brazil.
   B Do my new glasses fit all right?
   C You had ought to wear a bicycle helmet.
   D Vincent hurt hisself when he fell.

2. A Shannon Lindstrom became a artist at an early age.
   B My locker smells badly!
   C How come Rover barks at squirrels?
   D Elsa plays the piano better than I do.

3. A Several times a year, a snake sheds it's outer skin.
   B Everyone accept Amy ate a healthy breakfast.
   C Aren't you supposed to lock the door?
   D Them beautiful robes were made in Oman.

4. A Russian ain't the main language spoken in Armenia.
   B Would you divide the crackers among the four children, Paul?
   C I played bad because my hand hurt.
   D Let's have a snack and than do our homework.

5. A The children are already for the party.
   B Whose the prime minister of Japan?
   C There is your book!
   D A limerick is when a funny five-line poem has a certain rhyme pattern.

6.
- **A** I can scarcely taste the garlic in the sauce.
- **B** Our friends the Kahns are celebrating because its Mr. and Mrs. Kahn's twentieth wedding anniversary.
- **C** Your next in line.
- **D** Mitchell must of been tired after the game.

7.
- **A** They're grandparents are visiting from Thailand.
- **B** My keys have to be somewheres in this room!
- **C** I can't hardly do fifty sit-ups.
- **D** A lot of my friends volunteer with the Special Olympics.

8.
- **A** I should of asked for help.
- **B** This here Moroccan stew is called *tajine*.
- **C** Yo-Yo Ma plays the cello well.
- **D** The people of Lithuania eat alot of potatoes.

9.
- **A** "Poem" by Langston Hughes is sort of sad.
- **B** The airport is a long way from our house.
- **C** The country of Myanmar use to be known as Burma.
- **D** Are we allowed to go inside of the space shuttle?

10.
- **A** Where is the National Museum of the American Indian at?
- **B** This year less students joined the running club.
- **C** The pencil rolled off the table.
- **D** In today's meet Esta will try and break the school's long jump record.

Capital Letters: Rules for Capitalization

for CHAPTER 11 *page 238*

CHAPTER TEST

DIRECTIONS Read each set of sentences below. Three of the sentences in each set have errors in capitalization; one sentence is written correctly. Choose the sentence that is written correctly, with NO ERRORS in capitalization.

EXAMPLE

1. A Do you know if United Nations day is on October 24?
   B Many hopi still live in villages in northeastern Arizona.
   C Origami is a popular art among the japanese.
   D To raise money for cancer research, Terry Fox ran the Marathon of Hope.

   Answer Ⓐ Ⓑ Ⓒ ●

---

1. A our dog's name is Zelda.
   B We just bought an Epson® printer.
   C Did your ancestors fight in the Civil war?
   D Charlie and i are tennis partners.

2. A We are taking swimming lessons at the ymca.
   B My favorite actor is tom hanks.
   C Oops! I spilled water on my keyboard.
   D do you write poetry?

3. A The Aztec built decorative stone sculptures.
   B About 85 percent of Burma's people practice buddhism.
   C Not much rain falls in the country of yemen.
   D The *titanic* sank on its first voyage.

4. A Olia attends the russian classical dance school.
   B The sacred book of Islam is the Koran.
   C I would like a new pair of puma® running shoes.
   D A famous painting by Paul Cézanne is *the clockmaker*.

5. A Every morning grandma Winans rides her bicycle.
   B How long did queen Salote Tupou rule Tonga?
   C The flutist James Galway will perform tonight.
   D Today our art appreciation II class is going on a field trip.

for CHAPTER 11 page 238 continued **CHAPTER TEST**

6. A Is Jupiter the fifth planet from the sun?
   B The women's national basketball association was created in 1997.
   C Kevin just finished reading *dragon's gate* by Laurence Yep.
   D Did you invite dr. Tipton to speak to our class?

7. A How bright the Moon is tonight!
   B Will Principal Susan L. Rodgers attend the banquet?
   C As a missionary, she worked hard to spread her christian beliefs.
   D Does your family celebrate hanukkah?

8. A When was the panama canal built?
   B I always laugh when I read the comic strip *jump start*.
   C Sylvia Zamora, our Class President, is a good speaker.
   D The first African American to serve on the Supreme Court was Justice Thurgood Marshall.

9. A Ohio got its name from an Iroquois word for "something great."
   B During the middle ages, very wealthy landowners often lived in castles.
   C I would like you to meet my Cousin Molly.
   D Maia Wojciechowska won a newbery medal for *Shadow of a Bull*.

10. A Will you speak to the press now, mayor?
    B This portuguese soup is delicious.
    C How exciting the hands-on science exhibits are at the new Museum!
    D Do we have a test in math tomorrow?

Punctuation: End Marks, Commas, Semicolons, Colons

DIRECTIONS Read each set of items below. Three of the items in each set have errors in punctuation; one item is written correctly. Choose the item that is written correctly, with NO ERRORS in punctuation.

EXAMPLE

1. A Will Mr T K Blake be here today?
   B Yes I would like to taste the tofu curry.
   C Watch the graceful, athletic movements of the dance troupe.
   D How exciting that movie was

   Answer   ●

1. A Is Costa Rica in Central America.
   B Please read us a story
   C Tonya is on the yearbook staff, she is a good photographer.
   D Dear Senator Gonzales:

2. A Well I guess you can go to the movie.
   B Virginia Beach, Virginia, is a popular vacation spot.
   C Does the bus pick you up at 7;15?
   D The Sun Dance was an important religious celebration among the Arapaho Cheyenne Cree Pawnee and Sioux.

3. A Look at that gigantic fish!
   B A group of lions is called a "pride".
   C The first written laws were created in Babylonia around 2100 B C.
   D I live in Rhode Island the smallest state in the United States.

4. A Dear Uncle Carlos:
   B Be careful crossing the street; look both ways first.
   C I wake up at 7;00 every morning.
   D My favorite snack is a crunchy, juicy, apple.

5. A What a spectacular play that was.
   B Ginger, cinnamon, and cumin are common spices.
   C Tony bought a videotape I bought a CD.
   D Dr Dean Ornish has written many books about good health.

for CHAPTER 12 page 262 continued

CHAPTER TEST

6. A He ran up the steps, opened the door, and called my name.
   B Is your new address 211 Daisy Lane; Davis; WV 26260?
   C Andy Bergent a talented violinist is part of the Slovenia Trio.
   D Because I went to soccer practice I did not see the play last night.

7. A How obedient your dog is?
   B Tokyo has several art museums, my favorite is the Japan Folk Crafts Museum.
   C These are the herbs we planted rosemary, basil, and thyme.
   D May I, Mrs. Costas, collect the papers?

8. A Who holds the world record in the mile run!
   B We wanted to visit the aquarium but it was closed for repairs.
   C The following countries begin with the letter *C:* Cambodia, Chile, Cuba, and China.
   D Suzi where are the scissors?

9. A Tito Beltran is a young, talented opera tenor from Chile.
   B Tim jumped up from his seat, and ran to the window.
   C We are going to Big Bend a national park on the Rio Grande.
   D Is a giraffe the world's tallest animal.

10. A My nephew was born on April 6, 1999 in Mexico City.
    B Popular sports at our school are basketball, and soccer.
    C Ana, would you read aloud the poem by Naomi Shihab Nye?
    D For every swim meet you will need: goggles, a towel, and a swimsuit.

Punctuation: Underlining (Italics), Quotation Marks, Apostrophes, Hyphens, Parentheses

for CHAPTER 13 *page 288* — **CHAPTER TEST**

DIRECTIONS Read each set of sentences below. Three of the sentences in each set have errors in punctuation; one sentence is written correctly. Choose the sentence that is written correctly, with NO ERRORS in punctuation.

EXAMPLE

1. **A** I am trying to use fewer *and*s in my writing.
   B Abraham is learning the folk song "My Darling Clementine."
   C Can lemon juice harm teeths' enamel?
   D Julie added, "Every night Grandma says, "Early to bed, early to rise"."

   Answer Ⓐ ●B Ⓒ Ⓓ

---

1. **A** Someone's papers (I hope they are not mine) are blowing away!
   B Leroy said "that our new uniforms have arrived."
   C Emily cant find her pet iguana.
   D "How cold this room feels"! complained Mother.

2. **A** Pat Mora uses imagery in her poem Petals.
   B "I collect key chains," explained Martha.
   C Who's red sweater is this?
   D "Tomorrow, said Katerina, my aunt will arrive from Cuba."

3. **A** His' favorite hobby is playing backgammon.
   B "Would you like to use my CD-ROM encyclopedia?" "It has great pictures!" said Carla.
   C Michelle spells her name with two *l*'s.
   D The drama club is performing the play Fiddler on the Roof.

4. **A** Father said, "look at today's headlines!"
   B Thirty five girls are trying out for the cheerleading squad this year.
   C Theyre learning to make American Indian smudge sticks.
   D Oscar's hand-woven hat is from Bolivia.

5. **A** The mens' volleyball league plays on Tuesday.
   B I like the painting *Guardian of the Valley* by John Clark.
   C "Shirley Chisholm," explained Mona, "Was the first African American woman to serve in Congress."
   D The photo album the one with the globe on the cover is theirs'.

GO ON

for **CHAPTER 13** page 288 continued **CHAPTER TEST**

6. A "All aboard!" yelled the captain.
   B "In Japan we often eat seaweed and raw fish", explained Daisuke.
   C We have to drive only twenty five more miles.
   D Will our science test cover the chapter The Simplest Living Things?

7. A I enjoyed reading the book "The Land I Lost: Adventures of a Boy in Vietnam."
   B Weve been here for only five minutes!
   C Juan asked "Have you ever been to the World of Scouting Museum?"
   D The racers' wheelchairs were inspected for safety.

8. A Ladie's hats are on sale today.
   B My favorite story by Sandra Cisneros is *Eleven*.
   C Both of the girls' backpacks have broken zippers.
   D Mr. Eudaley said, "I became a librarian because I love books".

9. A Grandpa said, "I will tell you a Coyote story. Coyote is a trickster character from American Indian folk tales."
   B I would like to hear everyones' opinion.
   C I wonder why Jasper wasnt at practice today.
   D "I am building a bookcase." said Sara proudly.

10. A "Did Coach Stein say, "The bus leaves at noon?"
    B The magazine American Girl has stories, tips, and games.
    C Did you hear Janet say that Grandmother Jefferson's favorite winter treat is baked apple with cinnamon sprinkled on top?
    D Elton said, "This documentary about *Apollo 13* is exciting!"

Spelling: Improving Your Spelling

for CHAPTER 14 page 316

CHAPTER TEST

DIRECTIONS Read each set of sentences below. The underlined word is spelled incorrectly in three of the sentences in each set; in one of the sentences, the underlined word is spelled correctly. Choose the sentence in which the underlined word is spelled CORRECTLY.

EXAMPLE

1. A   The tribes' leaders reached an agreement.
   B   Our community has many volunteer organizationes.
   C   The capitol of Syria is Damascus.
   D   How many words did you mispell?

   Answer (A) (B) (C) (D)

1. A   Go threw the lobby and turn left.
   B   Are those hand-woven woolen rugs from Ecuador?
   C   I hurryed to catch the bus.
   D   We are planing a surprise party for Olivia.

2. A   Do you feel sleepier after drinking warm milk?
   B   There home in the Philippines is made from bamboo.
   C   I picked you a bouquet of daisyes.
   D   The climb to the top of Mount Everest is two dangerous.

3. A   Please help me dry the dishs.
   B   Would you like to here Addie play the bagpipes?
   C   Our school principle was an Olympic swimmer.
   D   What a lovable puppy that is!

4. A   Mom says that life is one long search for happyness.
   B   Our class has two pet mouses named Yes and No.
   C   In Japan, elders are treated with great respect.
   D   You're costume design won first prize!

5. A   I am hopeing to see the Kodo drummers perform tonight.
   B   How many s's are in *Mississippi*?
   C   Please be carful with Father's Burmese harp.
   D   Let's stay altogether at the museum.

GO ON

Chapter Tests 27

for CHAPTER 14 page 316 continued **CHAPTER TEST**

6. A We are taking used <u>toyes</u> to the homeless shelter.
    B I <u>beleive</u> that recycling is important.
    C Kwanzaa, a weeklong African American holiday, was <u>developed</u> by Maulana Karenga.
    D Bonnie competes in <u>rodeoes</u> throughout the Southwest.

7. A We made purple dye with <u>blackberries</u>.
    B Roberto has many model <u>spacecraft's</u> hanging from his ceiling.
    C The <u>countrys</u> that border Nicaragua are Honduras and Costa Rica.
    D <u>Its</u> not too late to enter the contest.

8. A Seattle was named for the Salish leader <u>Cheif</u> Sealth.
    B Merino <u>sheeps</u> are raised for their fine wool.
    C These folk tales have strong, kind <u>heros</u>.
    D The country of Qatar is mostly a flat, stony <u>desert</u>.

9. A Both <u>patios</u> are made of concrete.
    B We were <u>unncertain</u> which road to take.
    C The United Nations works for world <u>piece</u>.
    D I am <u>finaly</u> finished with the yard work!

10. A The Richters make a type of sausage with grated <u>potatos</u>.
    B My little sister is so proud of her <u>loose</u> tooth!
    C These <u>waltzs</u> were composed by Peter Ilich Tchaikovsky.
    D In 1920, <u>womans</u> of the United States gained the right to vote.

NAME _____ CLASS _____ DATE _____ SCORE _____

for **CHAPTER 15** page 346

CHAPTER TEST

Correcting Common Errors: Key Language Skills Review

DIRECTIONS Read each set of sentences below. Three of the sentences in each set contain common errors in language skills; one sentence is written correctly. Choose the sentence that is written correctly, with NO ERRORS in key language skills.

> **EXAMPLE**
>
> 1. **A** Everyone brought his or her own lunch.
>   **B** Neither John nor Ray will enter their poem in the contest.
>   **C** None of the yogurt has fruit in them.
>   **D** Because of today's heat, few of the runners will better her own times.
>
>   Answer (Ⓐ) Ⓑ Ⓒ Ⓓ

1. **A** Attended school in Egypt for six months.
   B A turtle's shell is very strong it contains approximately sixty bones.
   C Because I have never seen snow.
   D What an interesting story you told!

2. **A** The children of Israel plants trees for the Tu Bishvat holiday.
   B Everyone in Rosa's family speak Spanish.
   C Books or a toy keeps my little brother busy.
   D He don't remember his e-mail address.

3. **A** I have rode the Narrow Gauge Railroad from Durango to Silverton.
   B Amelia passed the ball, and Julie catches it.
   C Have you drunk eight glasses of water today?
   D Our city has risen over a million dollars for low-income housing.

4. **A** Her and me will help weed the garden.
   B The actor who played the part of Romeo was he.
   C Grandma showed Ana and I a beautiful pearl mosqueta from Panama.
   D Us boys want to see more paintings by Edmund Dulac.

5. **A** We priced two skateboards, and this one is cheaper.
   B The most largest reptile is the saltwater crocodile.
   C I haven't read neither of those books by Isaac Bashevis Singer.
   D I bought a shawl in Mexico with a colorful pattern.

GO ON

Chapter Tests 29

6. **A** We should of asked Kim to referee the game.
  B I will try and make enchiladas for supper.
  C Leo has already turned in his science project.
  D After that long hike, I am kind of tired.

7. **A** Is the metropolitan museum of art in New York City?
  B The traditional dress for Mongolian men and women is a long robe over heavy trousers and knee-high boots.
  C Do you have an appointment with dr. p. Patel?
  D The Secretary took notes during the meeting.

8. **A** Mrs. T. J. Tipton will be the new assistant principal.
  B The hand-woven, colorful, basket is from Senegal.
  C Wash your hands Megan before eating your snack.
  D Because the African drummers are each playing a different rhythm the music is called *polyrhythmic*.

9. **A** Have you ever read the book "Julie of the Wolves" by Jean Craighead George?
  B Every morning Mr. Borges (He is my favorite teacher.) says to our class, "Welcome to a wonderful, new day"!
  C "Charge the goal," instructed Coach Simms, "Every time our team shoots the ball."
  D Miss Chang said, "For homework please read the Hmong folk tale 'The Story of the Owl.'"

10. **A** Did Mary Azarian recieve the Caldecott Medal in 1999?
  B Large kangaroos can jump thirty feet in a single leap!
  C The locateion of our clubhouse is secret.
  D Please correct all mispelled words.

for **CHAPTER 16** page 384

CHAPTER TEST

Writing Effective Sentences

DIRECTIONS Read each question below. Then, choose the answer option that best answers the question.

EXAMPLE

1. What is the best way to combine these two sentences? *Sarah wrote a letter to her aunt. Sarah mailed a letter to her aunt.*
   A Sarah writing and mailing a letter to her aunt.
   B Sarah wrote a letter to her aunt because she mailed a letter to her aunt.
   C Sarah wrote a letter to her aunt, Sarah mailed a letter to her aunt.
   D Sarah wrote and mailed a letter to her aunt.
   Answer   Ⓓ

---

1. What is missing from the following? *The birds eagerly around the fresh bird food.*
   A Subject
   B Verb
   C Subject and verb
   D Direct object

2. What is the best way to combine these two sentences? *The divers are preparing their gear. They are preparing their gear in the boat.*
   A The divers are preparing their gear they are in the boat.
   B The divers are preparing their gear, but they are in the boat.
   C In the boat, preparing their gear.
   D The divers are preparing their gear in the boat.

3. What is the best way to combine these two sentences? *Last night we watched some fireworks. The fireworks were a thrill.*
   A Last night we watched some thrilling fireworks.
   B Last night we watched some fireworks and they were a thrill.
   C Last night we watched some fireworks, or they were a thrill.
   D Last night we watched some fireworks, but they were a thrill.

4. What is the best way to combine the following? *Next month Ms. Dunn will teach us. About solids and liquids.*
   A Next month Ms. Dunn about solids and liquids.
   B Next month Ms. Dunn will teach us about solids and liquids.
   C Next month Ms. Dunn will teach us, she will teach us about solids and liquids.
   D Next month Ms. Dunn will teach us, and about solids and liquids.

5. Why does the following word group need to be revised? *Wandered and wandered until sundown.*
   A It has no subject.
   B It has no verb.
   C It is a stringy sentence.
   D It is a run-on sentence.

6. What is the best way to combine these two sentences? *The daffodils are blooming. The tulips are blooming.*
   A The daffodils are blooming, the tulips are blooming.
   B The daffodils are blooming, but tulips are blooming.
   C The daffodils are blooming the tulips are blooming.
   D The daffodils and tulips are blooming.

Chapter Tests

for CHAPTER 16 page 384 continued
CHAPTER TEST

7. What is the best way to combine these two sentences? *Our club raised some money. We were unable to purchase the new equipment.*
   A With a comma and the conjunction *and*
   B With a comma and the conjunction *but*
   C With a comma and the conjunction *or*
   D Remove the period after *money*

8. To combine the following sentences, which word from the second sentence should be inserted into the first sentence? *Mr. Lopez looked at the storm clouds and scowled. His scowl was fierce.*
   A scowl + *ing*
   B fierce + *ing*
   C fierce + *ly*
   D scowl + *ly*

9. What kind of word group is this? *Our landlord washed the walls, and our landlord had the carpets cleaned, and he even washed all of the windows.*
   A Stringy sentence
   B Sentence fragment
   C Run-on sentence
   D Complex sentence

10. What is the best word to use to combine the following sentences? *I am very interested in trees. I don't know much about them.*
    A After
    B Until
    C Whose
    D Although

11. What is the best way to revise this sentence? *The science teacher showed us an experiment then she asked us to do our own.*
    A The science teacher showed us an experiment. Then she asked us to do our own.
    B The science teacher showed us an experiment, then she asked us to do our own.
    C The science teacher showed us an experiment then the science teacher asked us to do our own.
    D The science teacher showed us an experiment after she asked us to do our own.

12. What is the best way to combine these two sentences? *The puppy barked. The puppy barked so that it could get our attention.*
    A The puppy barked then he got our attention.
    B The puppy barked, he got our attention.
    C The puppy barked to get our attention.
    D The puppy barked the puppy got our attention.

13. Why does the following sentence need to be revised? *Teresa has a new job, she babysits on Saturday nights.*
    A It has no subject.
    B It links two complete ideas with a comma.
    C It has no verb.
    D It is made up of two sentence fragments.

GO ON

HOLT HANDBOOK | Introductory Course

for **CHAPTER 16** page 384 continued

CHAPTER TEST

> Celia steadily swam two laps. Celia swam using a kickboard. Then she rested at the edge of the pool. The swimming coach spoke to her. The swimming coach is Mr. Aaron. Mr. Aaron told Celia to warm up, he told her to pace herself.

14. To combine the first two sentences from the paragraph, what word group from the second sentence should be added to the first sentence?
  A Celia swam
  B swam using
  C using a kickboard
  D a kickboard

15. The final sentence of the paragraph is a run-on sentence. What is the best way to revise it?
  A When Mr. Aaron told Celia to warm up and to pace herself.
  B Mr. Aaron told Celia to warm up, or he told her to pace herself.
  C Mr. Aaron told Celia to warm up. And told her to pace herself.
  D Mr. Aaron told Celia to warm up and to pace herself.

16. What is the best way to combine these two sentences from the paragraph? *The swimming coach spoke to her. The swimming coach is Mr. Aaron.*
  A The swimming coach and Mr. Aaron spoke to her.
  B The swimming coach spoke to her and Mr. Aaron.
  C The swimming coach is Mr. Aaron, he spoke to her.
  D The swimming coach, Mr. Aaron, spoke to her.

> Tim may be awarded a prize. Pat may be awarded a prize. An assembly will be held during first period. It will be an all-school assembly.

17. What is the best way to combine these two sentences from the paragraph? *Tim may be awarded a prize. Pat may be awarded a prize.*
  A Tim may be awarded a prize, Pat may be awarded a prize.
  B Tim and Pat awarded a prize.
  C Tim and Pat may be awarded a prize.
  D Tim may be awarded a prize Pat may be awarded a prize.

18. What is the best way to combine these two sentences from the paragraph? *An assembly will be held during first period. It will be an all-school assembly.*
  A An all-school assembly will be held during first period.
  B An assembly will be held during first period, it will be an all-school assembly.
  C An assembly, an all-school assembly, during first period.
  D An all-school assembly during first period.

Chapter Tests

for **CHAPTER 16** page 384 continued

CHAPTER TEST

19. What would be the best revision for this sentence? *When warm weather comes, my grandfather thinks about baseball, but I think about basketball and the basketball season lasts through spring, and there is always basketball on television.*

   A When warm weather comes, my grandfather thinks about baseball, and I think about basketball. Because the basketball season lasts through spring and there is always basketball on television.

   B When warm weather comes, my grandfather thinks about baseball, but I think about basketball because the basketball season lasts through spring there is always basketball on television.

   C When warm weather comes, my grandfather thinks about baseball, but I think about basketball. The basketball season lasts through spring, and there is always basketball on television.

   D When warm weather comes, my grandfather thinks about baseball. But I think about basketball, the basketball season lasts through spring because there is always basketball on television.

20. What kind of sentence is this? *Some people are surprised to learn that Sacramento is the capital of the state of California.*
   A a stringy sentence
   B a sentence fragment
   C a run-on sentence
   D a correct sentence

Answer Key

A black box around an answer choice indicates the correct answer. The information in parentheses to the right of each answer choice indicates the rule number(s) or concept(s) in the *Holt Handbook* to which the answer choice corresponds.

Chapter 1
The Sentence (Subject and Predicate, Kinds of Sentences), p. 1

1. A (1c)
   B (1d)
   C (1f)
   D (1e)

2. A (1a)
   B (1c)
   C (1b)
   D (1d)

3. A (1e)
   B (1d)
   C (1a)
   D (1b)

4. **A** (1g)
   B (1c)
   C (1d)
   D (1f)

5. A (1e)
   B (1b)
   C (1c)
   D (1a)

6. A (1d)
   B (1b)
   C (1g)
   D (1f)

7. **A** (1k)
   B (1i)
   C (1j)
   D (1h)

8. A (1k)
   B (1h)
   C (1i)
   D (1j)

9. **A** (1i)
   B (1j)
   C (1k)
   D (1h)

10. A (1k)
    B (1i)
    C (1h)
    D (1j)

Chapter 2
Parts of Speech Overview (Noun, Pronoun, Adjective), p. 3

1. A (2a)
   B (2b)
   C (2a)
   D (2c)

2. **A** (2b)
   B (2a)
   C (2c)
   D (2a)

3. A (2c)
   B (2c)
   C (2a)
   D (2a)

4. A (2a)
   B (2c)
   C (2a)
   D (2b)

5. A (2a)
   B (2b)
   C (2c)
   D (2c)

6. A (2a)
   B (2a)
   C (2c)
   D (2b)

7. A (2a)
   B (2b)
   C (2c)
   D (2c)

8. **A** (2c)
   B (2b)
   C (2c)
   D (2a)

9. A (2b)
   B (2a)
   C (2a)
   D (2c)

10. A (2a)
    B (2c)
    C (2b)
    D (2c)

Chapter 3
Parts of Speech Overview (Verb, Adverb, Preposition, Conjunction, Interjection), p. 5

1. A (3b, f)
   B (3d)
   C (3c, f)
   D (3a)

2. A (3a)
   B (3a)
   C (3d)
   D (3b)

3. **A** (3a)
   B (3a)
   C (3e)
   D (3d)

4. A (3b)
   B (3e)
   C (3d)
   D (3a)

5. A (3e)
   B (3a)
   C (3a)
   D (3b)

6. A (3c)
   B (3a)
   C (3d)
   D (3b)

7. A (3c)
   B (3a)
   C (3e)
   D (3d)

8. A (3a)
   B (3a)
   C (3d)
   D (3a)

9. **A** (3c)
   B (3d)
   C (3a)
   D (3e)

10. A (3a)
    B (3a)
    C (3a)
    D (3a)

A black box around an answer choice indicates the correct answer. The information in parentheses to the right of each answer choice indicates the rule number(s) or concept(s) in the *Holt Handbook* to which the answer choice corresponds.

Chapter 4
The Phrase and the Clause (Prepositional Phrases, Independent and Subordinate Clauses, Sentence Structure), p. 7

1. **A** (4c)
   B (4d)
   C (4h)
   D (4i)

2. A (4g)
   B (4d)
   C (4f)
   D (4c)

3. A (4h)
   B (4c)
   C (4d)
   D (4i)

4. A (4c)
   B (4d)
   C (4f)
   D (4g)

5. **A** (4b)
   B (4f)
   C (4h)
   D (4i)

6. A (4b)
   B (4h)
   C (4f)
   D (4i)

7. **A** (4k)
   B (4j)
   C (4m)
   D (4l)

8. A (4m)
   B (4k)
   C (4j)
   D (4l)

9. A (4j)
   B (4l)
   C (4k)
   D (4m)

10. A (4j)
    B (4m)
    C (4k)
    D (4l)

Chapter 5
Complements (Direct and Indirect Objects, Subject Complements), p. 9

1. A (5b)
   B (5e)
   C (5c)
   D (5f)

2. A (5e)
   B (5f)
   C (5b)
   D (5c)

3. A (5b)
   B (5e)
   C (5c)
   D (5f)

4. A (5f)
   B (5c)
   C (5e)
   D (5b)

5. **A** (5e)
   B (5b)
   C (5c)
   D (5f)

6. A (5f)
   B (5b)
   C (5e)
   D (5c)

7. **A** (5c)
   B (5b)
   C (5f)
   D (5e)

8. A (5f)
   B (5c)
   C (5b)
   D (5e)

9. A (5c)
   B (5b)
   C (5e)
   D (5f)

10. A (5e)
    B (5b)
    C (5f)
    D (5c)

Chapter 6
Agreement (Subject and Verb, Pronoun and Antecedent), p. 11

1. A (6b[1])
   B (6b[2], e)
   C (6h)
   D (6o[5])

2. **A** (6b[2])
   B (6k, l, m)
   C (6b[2], k)
   D (6o[3])

3. A (6b[2], e)
   B (6b[1])
   C (6b[2], g)
   D (6o[4])

4. A (6b[2])
   B (6b[2], f)
   C (6b[2], k)
   D (6b[1], h)

5. **A** (6o[4])
   B (6b[1])
   C (6b[2], c)
   (D) (6b[2], g)

6. A (6b[2])
   B (6b[2], e)
   C (6o[1])
   D (6m, l)

7. A (6b[1], d)
   B (6b[2], g)
   C (6o[1])
   D (6b[2])

8. **A** (6l)
   B (6b[1], d)
   C (6b[2], c)
   D (6b[2], g,l)

9. A (6o[5])
   B (6o[2])
   C (6b[2], e)
   D (6n, o[1])

10. A (6o[4])
    B (6b[2], c)
    C (6b[1], d)
    D (6j)

Chapter 7
Using Verbs Correctly (Principal Parts, Regular and Irregular Verbs, Tense), p. 13

1. A (7c)
   B (7b)
   C (7d, *sit/set*)
   D (7c)

A black box around an answer choice indicates the correct answer. The information in parentheses to the right of each answer choice indicates the rule number(s) or concept(s) in the *Holt Handbook* to which the answer choice corresponds.

2. **A** (7d, *lie/lay*)
   B (7c)
   C (7c)
   D (7b)

3. A (*rise/raise*)
   B (7b)
   C (*sit/set*)
   D (7e)

4. A (7c)
   B (7e)
   C (7c)
   D (*rise/raise*)

5. **A** (7b)
   B (7c)
   C (7c)
   D (7d, *rise/raise*)

6. A (7c)
   B (*lie/lay*)
   C (7c)
   D (7e)

7. A (7c)
   B (*sit/set*)
   C (7c)
   D (*rise/raise*)

8. A (7c)
   B (*sit/set*)
   C (*rise/raise*)
   D (7e)

9. **A** (7b)
   B (7c)
   C (*lie/lay*)
   D (7e)

10. A (7b)
    B (7d, *sit/set*)
    C (*lie/lay*)
    D (7c)

Chapter 8
Using Pronouns Correctly (Subject and Object Forms), p. 15

1. A (8a)
   B (8c)
   C (8e)
   D (8d)

2. A (*pronouns with appositives*)
   B (8a)
   C (8d)
   D (8b)

3. **A** (*who/whom*)
   B (8d)
   C (8a)
   D (8c)

4. A (8c)
   B (8b)
   C (8d)
   D (8d)

5. A (*who/whom*)
   B (8e)
   C (8a)
   D (8b)

6. A (8d)
   B (*pronouns with appositives*)
   C (*who/whom*)
   D (8c)

7. **A** (8b)
   B (8c)
   C (8e)
   D (*pronouns with appositives*)

8. A (8c)
   B (8e)
   C (8c)
   D (8a)

9. **A** (*pronouns with appositives*)
   B (8b)
   C (8e)
   D (8d)

10. A (*who/whom*)
    B (8b)
    C (8a)
    D (8c)

Chapter 9
Using Modifiers Correctly (Comparison and Placement), p. 17

1. **A** (9d)
   B (9a, b)
   C (9g)
   D (9c[3], f)

2. A (9g)
   B (9c[3], f)
   C (9d)
   D (9c[3])

3. A (9d)
   B (9a, h)
   C (9c[2])
   D (9c[3], f)

4. A (9c[3])
   B (9d)
   C (9a, b)
   D (9g)

5. A (9a, b)
   B (9a, h)
   C (9c[3])
   D (9c[2])

6. A (9g)
   B (9a, h)
   C (9c[2], f)
   D (9d)

7. A (9c[2], f)
   B (9g)
   C (9d)
   D (9a, h)

8. A (9a, h)
   B (9g)
   C (9b, h)
   D (9d)

9. **A** (9c[2])
   B (9a, h)
   C (9c[2])
   D (9c[3])

10. **A** (9a, h)
    B (9c[2])
    C (9g)
    D (9a, h)

A black box around an answer choice indicates the correct answer. The information in parentheses to the right of each answer choice indicates the rule number(s) or concept(s) in the *Holt Handbook* to which the answer choice corresponds.

Chapter 10
A Glossary of Usage (Common Usage Problems), p. 19

1. A (ain't)
   B (all right)
   C (had ought, hadn't ought)
   D (hisself, theirself, theirselves)

2. A (a, an)
   B (bad, badly)
   C (how come)
   D (than, then)

3. A (its, it's)
   B (accept, except)
   C (suppose to, supposed to)
   D (them)

4. A (ain't)
   B (between, among)
   C (bad, badly)
   D (than, then)

5. A (already, all ready)
   B (whose, who's)
   C (their, there, they're)
   D (when, where)

6. **A** (hardly, scarcely)
   B (its, it's)
   C (your, you're)
   D (might of, must of)

7. A (their, there, they're)
   B (somewheres)
   C (hardly, scarcely)
   D (a lot)

8. A (should of)
   B (this here, that there)
   C (good, well)
   D (a lot)

9. A (kind of, sort of)
   B (way, ways)
   C (use to, used to)
   D (of)

10. A (at)
    B (fewer, less)
    C (of)
    D (try and)

Chapter 11
Capital Letters (Rules for Capitalization), p. 21

1. A (11a, d[1])
   B (11a, d[7])
   C (11a, d[5])
   D (11a, c)

2. A (11a, g)
   B (11a, d[1])
   C (11a, c)
   D (11a)

3. **A** (11a, d[6])
   B (11a, d[2], d[11])
   C (11a, d[2])
   D (11a, d[8])

4. A (11a, d[1], d[3])
   B (11a, d[11])
   C (11a, c, d[7])
   D (11a, d[1], h[4])

5. A (11a, h[3])
   B (11a, h[1], d[1], d[2])
   C (11a, d[1])
   D (11a, e)

6. **A** (11a, d[12])
   B (11a, d[3])
   C (11a, d[1], h[4])
   D (11a, h[1], d[1])

7. A (11a, d[12])
   B (11a, h[1], d[1])
   C (11a, f)
   D (11a, d[11])

8. A (11a, d[9])
   B (11a, c, h[4])
   C (11a, d[1], h[2])
   D (11a, d[6], d[3], h[1], d[1])

9. **A** (11a, d[2], f)
   B (11a, d[5])
   C (11a, c, h[3], d[1])
   D (11a, d[1], d[10], h[4])

10. A (11a, h[2])
    B (11a, f)
    C (11a, d)
    D (11a, e)

Chapter 12
Punctuation (End Marks, Commas, Semicolons, Colons), p. 23

1. A (12a, b)
   B (12d)
   C (12a, m)
   D (12p)

2. A (12a, j[1])
   B (12a, k[1])
   C (12b, o)
   D (12a, f)

3. **A** (12c)
   B (12a)
   C (12a, e)
   D (12a, i[1])

4. A (12k[2], p)
   B (12d, m)
   C (12a, o)
   D (12a, g, l)

5. A (12c)
   B (12a, f)
   C (12a, m)
   D (12a, e)

6. **A** (12a, f)
   B (12b, k[1])
   C (12a, i[1])
   D (12a, j[3])

7. A (12b, c)
   B (12a, m)
   C (12a, n)
   D (12b, i[2])

8. A (12b, c)
   B (12a, h)
   C (12a, n)
   D (12b, i[2])

A black box around an answer choice indicates the correct answer. The information in parentheses to the right of each answer choice indicates the rule number(s) or concept(s) in the *Holt Handbook* to which the answer choice corresponds.

9. **A** (12a, g)
   B (12a, h, l)
   C (12a, i[1])
   D (12a, b)

10. A (12a, k[1])
    B (12a, f, l)
    C (12b, i[2])
    D (12a, f, j[2], n)

Chapter 13
Punctuation (Underlining [Italics], Quotation Marks, Apostrophes, Hyphens, Parentheses), p. 25

1. **A** (13q, x)
   B (13c)
   C (13r)
   D (13c, d, h)

2. A (13l)
   B (13c, d, f[1], g)
   C (13r)
   D (13c, d, e, f[3], g)

3. A (13p)
   B (13c, d, f[1], h, j)
   C (13s)
   D (13a)

4. A (13f[2], c, d, h)
   B (13u)
   C (13r)
   D (13m, v)

5. A (13n)
   B (13a)
   C (13c, d, f[3], e)
   D (13p, x)

6. **A** (13c, d, f[1], h)
   B (13c, d, f[1], g)
   C (13u)
   D (13l)

7. A (13a, l)
   B (13r)
   C (13f[2], c, d, h)
   D (13o)

8. A (13o)
   B (13a, l)
   C (13o)
   D (13f[2], c, d, g)

9. **A** (13f[2], c, d, j, g)
   B (13q)
   C (13r)
   D (13c, d, f[1])

10. A (13c, f[2], k, h)
    B (13a)
    C (13t[1], t[3])
    D (13f[2], b, c, d, h)

Chapter 14
Spelling (Improving Your Spelling), p. 27

1. A (*threw, through*)
   B (14g)
   C (14f)
   D (14g)

2. **A** (14f)
   B (*their, there, they're*)
   C (14f)
   D (*to, too, two*)

3. A (14h[2])
   B (*hear, here*)
   C (*principal, principle*)
   D (14d)

4. A (14f)
   B (14h[7])
   C (14g)
   D (*your, you're*)

5. A (14d)
   B (14h[9])
   C (14e)
   D (*altogether, all together*)

6. A (14h[1])
   B (14a)
   C (14g)
   D (14h[5])

7. **A** (14h[3])
   B (14h[8])
   C (14h[3])
   D (*its, it's*)

8. A (14a)
   B (14h[8])
   C (14h[6])
   D (*desert, desert, dessert*)

9. **A** (14h[5])
   B (14b)
   C (*peace, piece*)
   D (14c)

10. A (14h[6])
    B (*loose, lose*)
    C (14h[2])
    D (14h[7])

Chapter 15
Correcting Common Errors (Key Language Skills Review), p. 29

1. A (1a, d)
   B (4k, 12m)
   C (1a, 4e, g)
   D (1k, 12c)

2. A (6b[2], c)
   B (6d)
   C (6j)
   D (6l, m)

3. A (7a, c, d)
   B (7e)
   C (7a, c, d)
   D (*rise/raise*)

4. A (8a)
   B (8b)
   C (8d)
   D (8a, *pronouns with appositives*)

5. **A** (9c[2])
   B (9c[3], f)
   C (9g)
   D (9h)

6. A (*should of* [Chapter 10])
   B (*try and* [Chapter 10])
   C (*already, all ready* [Chapter 10, Chapter 14])
   D (*kind of, sort of* [Chapter 10])

A black box around an answer choice indicates the correct answer. The information in parentheses to the right of each answer choice indicates the rule number(s) or concept(s) in the *Holt Handbook* to which the answer choice corresponds.

7. A (11a, d[9])
   B (11a, f)
   C (11a, h[1])
   D (11a, h[2])

8. **A** (12a, e)
   B (12g, 13v)
   C (12i[2])
   D (12j[3])

9. A (13a)
   B (13f[2], c, d, h, x)
   C (13c, f[3], e, g)
   D (13f[2], c, d, k, l, g)

10. A (14a)
    B (14h[1])
    C (14d)
    D (14b)

Chapter 16
Writing Effective Sentences, p. 31

1. **B** (recognizing fragments)

2. **D** (combining sentences by inserting word groups [prepositional phrase])

3. **A** (combining sentences by inserting words [changing a word by adding -*ing*])

4. **B** (revising fragments)

5. **A** (recognizing fragments)

6. **D** (combining sentences by joining subjects [with *and*])

7. **B** (combining complete sentences [to make a compound sentence])

8. **C** (combining sentences by inserting words [changing a word by adding -*ly*])

9. **A** (identifying stringy sentences)

10. **D** (combining complete sentences)

11. **A** (revising run-on sentences)

12. **C** (combining complete sentences by inserting word groups [infinitive phrase])

13. **B** (revising run-on sentences [comma splice])

14. **C** (combining sentences by inserting word groups [participial phrase])

15. **D** (revising run-on sentences [comma splice])

16. **D** (combining sentences by inserting word groups [appositive phrase])

17. **C** (combining sentences by joining subjects [with *and*])

18. **A** (combining sentences by inserting words)

19. **C** (revising stringy sentences)

20. **D** (recognizing correct sentences)

NAME _____ CLASS _____ DATE _____ SCORE _____

Answer Sheet

Chapter _____

1	Ⓐ	Ⓑ	Ⓒ	Ⓓ	11	Ⓐ	Ⓑ	Ⓒ	Ⓓ
2	Ⓐ	Ⓑ	Ⓒ	Ⓓ	12	Ⓐ	Ⓑ	Ⓒ	Ⓓ
3	Ⓐ	Ⓑ	Ⓒ	Ⓓ	13	Ⓐ	Ⓑ	Ⓒ	Ⓓ
4	Ⓐ	Ⓑ	Ⓒ	Ⓓ	14	Ⓐ	Ⓑ	Ⓒ	Ⓓ
5	Ⓐ	Ⓑ	Ⓒ	Ⓓ	15	Ⓐ	Ⓑ	Ⓒ	Ⓓ
6	Ⓐ	Ⓑ	Ⓒ	Ⓓ	16	Ⓐ	Ⓑ	Ⓒ	Ⓓ
7	Ⓐ	Ⓑ	Ⓒ	Ⓓ	17	Ⓐ	Ⓑ	Ⓒ	Ⓓ
8	Ⓐ	Ⓑ	Ⓒ	Ⓓ	18	Ⓐ	Ⓑ	Ⓒ	Ⓓ
9	Ⓐ	Ⓑ	Ⓒ	Ⓓ	19	Ⓐ	Ⓑ	Ⓒ	Ⓓ
10	Ⓐ	Ⓑ	Ⓒ	Ⓓ	20	Ⓐ	Ⓑ	Ⓒ	Ⓓ

Copyright © by Holt, Rinehart and Winston. All rights reserved.

Chapter Tests

CHAPTER 15

Correcting Common Errors
Test Answer Sheet

Most tests that are in a standardized format require that you use a No. 2 pencil. Each mark should be dark and should completely fill the intended oval. Be sure to erase completely any errors or stray marks. If you do not have a pencil, follow your teacher's instructions about how to mark your answers on this sheet.

1

Your Name: _____
(Print)   Last   First   M.I.

Signature: _____

Class: _____ Date: ___/___/___
(Print)   Month Day Year

2 Your Name

3 Date | **4 Grade** | **5 Age**

For each new section, begin with number 1. If a section has more answer spaces than questions, leave the extra spaces blank.

Grammar and Usage Test

Section 1

Section 2

Mechanics Test

Section 1

Section 2

42   HOLT HANDBOOK | Introductory Course